3-CHORD HYMNS
FOR GUITAR

ISBN 978-1-4584-2467-9

HAL•LEONARD®
CORPORATION

7777 W. BLUEMOUND RD. P.O. BOX 13819 MILWAUKEE, WI 53213

In Australia Contact:
Hal Leonard Australia Pty. Ltd.
4 Lentara Court
Cheltenham, Victoria, 3192 Australia
Email: ausadmin@halleonard.com.au

Visit Hal Leonard Online at
www.halleonard.com

Amazing Grace

Words by John Newton
Traditional American Melody

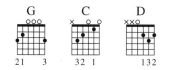

Additional Lyrics

2. 'Twas grace that taught my heart to fear,
And grace my fears relieved.
How precious did that grace appear
The hour I first believed.

3. Through many dangers, toils and snares,
I have already come.
'Tis grace hath brought me safe thus far,
And grace will lead me home.

4. The Lord has promised good to me,
His word my hope secures.
He will my shield and portion be
As long as life endures.

5. And when this flesh and heart shall fail,
And mortal life shall cease,
I shall possess within the veil
A life of joy and peace.

6. When we've been there ten thousand years,
Bright shining as the sun,
We've no less days to sing God's praise
Than when we first begun.

At the Cross

Words by Isaac Watts and Ralph E. Hudson
Music by Ralph E. Hudson

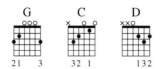

Additional Lyrics

2. Was it for crimes that I have done He groaned upon the tree?
   Amazing pity! Grace unknown! And love beyond degree!

3. Well might the sun in darkness hide and shut his glories in,
   When Christ, the mighty Maker, died for man, the creature's sin.

4. Thus might I hide my blushing face while Calv'ry's cross appears,
   Dissolve my heart in thankfulness and melt mine eyes to tears.

5. But drops of grief can ne'er repay the debt of love I owe.
   Here, Lord, I give myself away; 'tis all that I can do!

Battle Hymn of the Republic

Words by Julia Ward Howe
Music by William Steffe

Verse
Bright March

1. Mine eyes have seen the glo - ry of the com - ing of the Lord; He is
2.–4. *See additional lyrics*

tram - pling out the vin - tage where the grapes of wrath are stored. He hath

loosed the fate - ful light - ning of His ter - ri - ble swift sword; His

Chorus

truth is march - ing on. Glo - ry, glo - ry, hal - le - lu - jah!

Glo - ry, glo - ry, hal - le - lu - jah. Glo - ry, glo - ry, hal - le - lu - jah! His

1.–3.
truth is march - ing on.

4.
2. I have on.

Additional Lyrics

2. I have seen Him in the watchfires of a hundred circling camps;
   They have builded Him an altar in the evening dews and damps.
   I can read His righteous sentence by the dim and flaring lamps;
   His day is marching on.

3. He has sounded forth the trumpet that shall never sound retreat;
   He is sifting out the hearts of men before His judgment seat.
   O be swift, my soul, to answer Him! Be jubilant, my feet!
   Our God is marching on.

4. In the beauty of the lilies Christ was born across the sea,
   With a glory in His bosom that transfigures you and me.
   As He died to make men holy, let us die to make men free,
   While God is marching on.

Bringing in the Sheaves

Words by Knowles Shaw
Music by George A. Minor

Additional Lyrics

2. Sowing in the sunshine, sowing in the shadows,
   Fearing neither clouds nor winter's chilling breeze.
   By and by, the harvest and the labor ended,
   We shall come rejoicing, bringing in the sheaves.

3. Going forth with weeping, sowing for the Master,
   Though the loss sustained our spirit often grieves.
   When our weeping's over, He will bid us welcome;
   We shall come rejoicing, bringing in the sheaves.

Come, Christians, Join to Sing

Words by Christian Henry Bateman
Traditional Melody

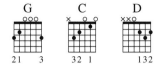

Additional Lyrics

2. Come, lift your hearts on high;
Alleluia! Amen!
Let praises fill the sky;
Alleluia! Amen!
He is our guide and friend;
To us He'll condescend.
His love shall never end:
Alleluia! Amen!

3. Praise yet our Christ again;
Alleluia! Amen!
Life shall not end the strain;
Alleluia! Amen!
On heaven's blissful shore
His goodness we'll adore,
Singing forevermore:
"Alleluia! Amen!"

Faith of Our Fathers

Words by Frederick W. Faber
Music by Henri F. Hemy and James G. Walton

Additional Lyrics

2. Faith of our fathers, faith and prayer
   Shall win all nations unto thee.
   And through the truth that comes from God,
   Mankind shall then be truly free.

3. Faith of our fathers, we will love
   Both friend and foe in all our strife;
   And preach thee, too, as love knows how,
   By kindly words and virtuous life.

For the Beauty of the Earth

Text by Folliot S. Pierpoint
Music by Conrad Kocher

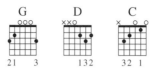

Additional Lyrics

2. For the wonder of each hour,
   Of the day and of the night,
   Hill and vale and tree and flow'r,
   Sun and moon and stars of light:

3. For the joy of ear and eye,
   For the heart and mind's delight,
   For the mystic harmony
   Linking sense to sound and sight:

4. For the joy of human love,
   Brother, sister, parent, child,
   Friends on earth and friends above,
   For all gentle thoughts and mild:

5. For Thy church that evermore
   Lifteth holy hands above,
   Off'ring up on every shore
   Her pure sacrifice of love:

6. For Thyself, best Gift Divine,
   To our race so freely giv'n,
   For that great, great love of Thine,
   Peace on earth and joy in heaven:

God of Grace and God of Glory

Text by Harry Emerson Fosdick
Music by John Hughes

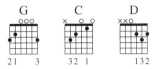

Additional Lyrics

2. Lo! The hosts of evil 'round us
   Scorn Thy Christ, assail His ways!
   From the fears that long have bound us,
   Free our hearts to faith and praise.
   Grant us wisdom, grant us courage,
   For the living of these days,
   For the living of these days.

3. Cure Thy children's warring madness,
   Bend our pride to Thy control.
   Shame our wanton, selfish gladness,
   Rich in things and poor in soul.
   Grant us wisdom, grant us courage,
   Lest we miss Thy kingdom's goal,
   Lest we miss Thy kingdom's goal.

4. Set our feet on lofty places,
   Gird our lives that they may be
   Armored with all Christ-like graces
   In the fight to set men free.
   Grant us wisdom, grant us courage,
   That we fail not man nor Thee,
   That we fail not man nor Thee.

I Sing the Mighty Power of God

Words by Isaac Watts
Music from *Gesangbuch der Herzogl*

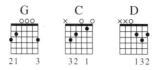

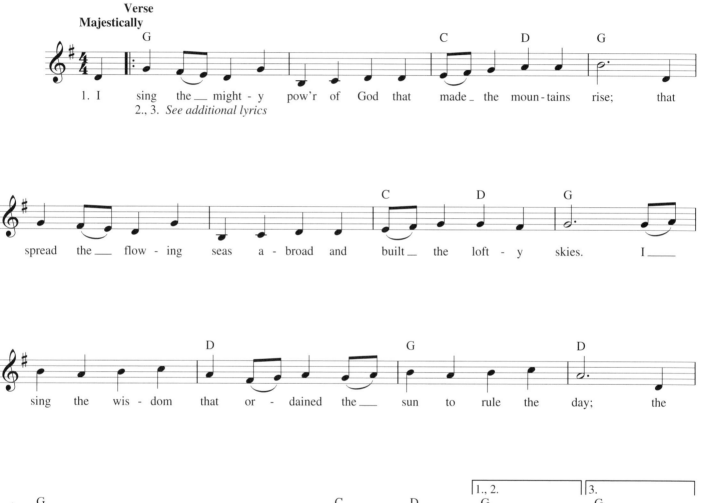

Verse
Majestically

1. I sing the ___ might - y pow'r of God that made ___ the moun - tains rise; that
2., 3. *See additional lyrics*

spread the ___ flow - ing seas a - broad and built ___ the loft - y skies. I ___

sing the wis - dom that or - dained the ___ sun to rule the day; the

moon shines ___ full at His com - mand, and all ___ the stars o - bey. 2. I there.

Additional Lyrics

2. I sing the goodness of the Lord that filled the earth with food;
   He formed the creatures with His word and then pronounced them good.
   Lord, how Thy wonders are displayed where'er I turn my eyes;
   If I survey the ground I tread, or gaze upon the skies!

3. There's not a plant or flow'r below but makes Thy glories known;
   And clouds arise, and tempests blow, by order from Thy throne.
   While all that borrows life from Thee is ever in Thy care,
   And ev'rywhere that we can be, Thou, God, art present there.

I Surrender All

Words by J.W. Van Deventer
Music by W.S. Weeden

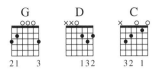

Additional Lyrics

2. All to Jesus I surrender; humbly at His feet I bow.
   Worldly pleasures all forsaken; take me, Jesus, take me now.

3. All to Jesus I surrender; make me, Savior, wholly Thine.
   Let me feel Thy Holy Spirit, truly know that Thou art mine.

4. All to Jesus I surrender; Lord, I give myself to Thee.
   Fill me with Thy love and power; let Thy blessing fall on me.

5. All to Jesus I surrender; now I feel the sacred flame.
   O the joy of full salvation! Glory, glory to His name!

Jesus, Keep Me Near the Cross

Words by Fanny J. Crosby
Music by William H. Doane

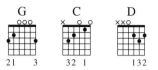

Additional Lyrics

2. Near the cross, a trembling soul,
   Love and mercy found me;
   There the Bright and Morning Star
   Sheds its beams around me.

3. Near the cross! O Lamb of God,
   Bring its scenes before me;
   Help me walk from day to day
   With its shadows o'er me.

4. Near the cross I'll watch and wait,
   Hoping, trusting ever,
   Till I reach the golden strand
   Just beyond the river.

Jesus Loves Me

Words by Anna Warner
Music by William Bradbury

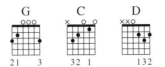

Additional Lyrics

2. Jesus loves me; He who died,
   Heaven's gates to open wide.
   He will wash away my sin,
   Let His little child come in.

3. Jesus loves me; loves me still,
   Though I'm very weak and ill.
   From His shining throne on high,
   Comes to watch me where I lie.

4. Jesus loves me; He will stay
   Close beside me all the way.
   If I love Him, when I die,
   He will take me home on high.

Joyful, Joyful, We Adore Thee

Words by Henry van Dyke
Music by Ludwig van Beethoven, melody from *Ninth Symphony*
Adapted by Edward Hodges

Additional Lyrics

2. All Thy works with joy surround Thee,
   Earth and heav'n reflect Thy rays.
   Stars and angels sing around Thee,
   Center of unbroken praise.
   Field and forest, vale and mountain,
   Flow'ry meadow, flashing sea,
   Chanting bird and flowing fountain
   Call us to rejoice in Thee.

3. Thou art giving and forgiving,
   Ever blessing, ever blest;
   Well-spring of the joy of living,
   Ocean depth of happy rest.
   Thou our Father, Christ our Brother,
   All who live in love are Thine.
   Teach us how to love each other,
   Lift us to the joy divine.

4. Mortals, join the happy chorus
   Which the morning stars began.
   Father-love is reigning o'er us,
   Brother-love binds man to man.
   Ever singing, march we onward,
   Victors in the midst of strife.
   Joyful music leads us sunward
   In the triumph song of life.

Leaning on the Everlasting Arms

Words by Elisha A. Hoffman
Music by Anthony J. Showalter

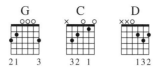

Verse
Bright Swing feel

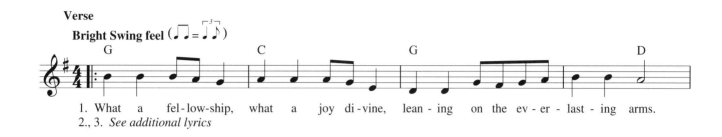

1. What a fel-low-ship, what a joy di-vine, lean-ing on the ev-er-last-ing arms.
2., 3. *See additional lyrics*

What a bless-ed-ness, what a peace is mine, lean-ing on the ev-er-last-ing arms.

Chorus

Lean-ing, lean-ing, safe and se-cure from all a-larms; Lean-ing,

lean-ing, lean-ing on the ev-er-last-ing arms. last-ing arms.

Additional Lyrics

2. Oh, how sweet to walk in this pilgrim way,
Leaning on the everlasting arms.
Oh, how bright the path grows from day to day.
Leaning on the everlasting arms.

3. What have I to dread, what have I to fear,
Leaning on the everlasting arms?
I have blessed peace with my Lord so near,
Leaning on the everlasting arms.

My Jesus, I Love Thee

Text by William R. Featherstone
Music by Adoniram J. Gordon

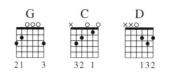

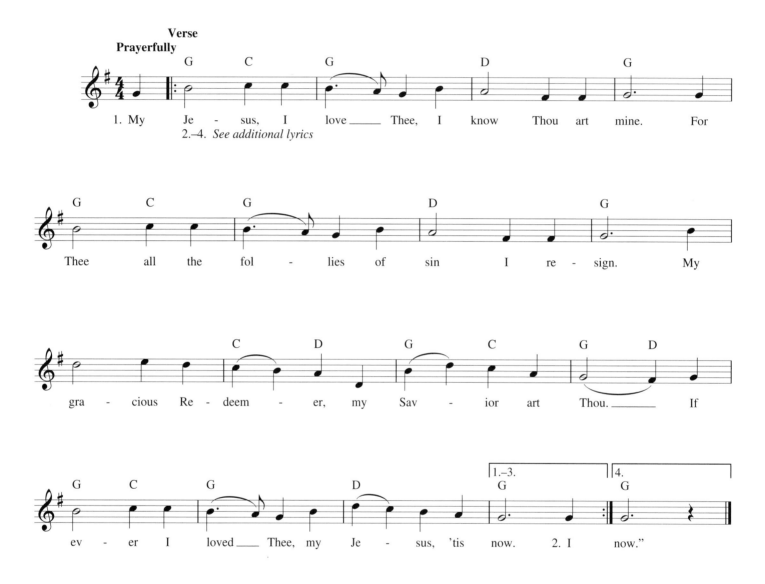

Additional Lyrics

2. I love Thee because Thou hast first loved me,
   And purchased my pardon on Calvary's tree.
   I love Thee for wearing the thorns on Thy brow.
   If ever I loved Thee, my Jesus, 'tis now.

3. I'll love Thee in life, I will love Thee in death,
   And praise Thee as long as Thou lendest me breath,
   And say when the death dew lies cold on my brow,
   "If ever I loved Thee, my Jesus, 'tis now."

4. In mansions of glory and endless delight,
   I'll ever adore Thee in heaven so bright.
   I'll sing with the glittering crown on my brow,
   "If ever I loved Thee, my Jesus, 'tis now."

Nearer, My God, to Thee

Text by Sarah F. Adams
Music by Lowell Mason

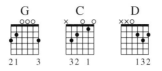

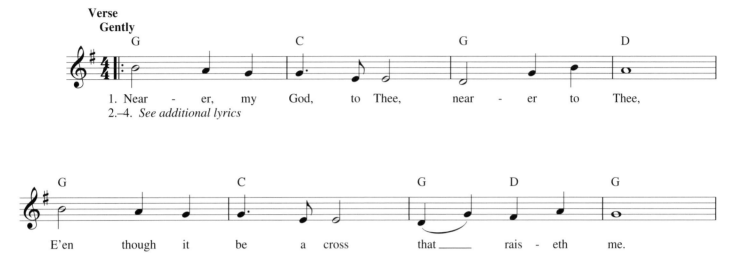

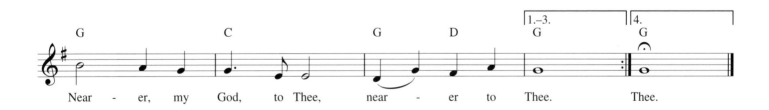

Additional Lyrics

2. Though, like the wanderer, the sun go down,
   Darkness be over me, my rest a stone;
   Yet in my dreams I'd be nearer, my God, to Thee.
   Nearer, my God, to Thee, nearer to Thee.

3. Then with my waking thoughts bright with Thy praise,
   Out of my stony griefs Bethel I'll raise;
   So by my woes to be nearer, my God, to Thee.
   Nearer, my God, to Thee, nearer to Thee.

4. Or if on joyful wing, cleaving the sky,
   Sun, moon and stars forgot, upward I fly;
   Still all my song shall be: nearer, my God, to Thee.
   Nearer, my God, to Thee, nearer to Thee.

O Worship the King

Words by Robert Grant
Music attributed to Johann Michael Haydn

Additional Lyrics

2. O tell of His might, O sing of His grace,
   Whose robe is the light, whose canopy, space.
   His chariots of wrath the deep thunderclouds form,
   And dark is His path on the wings of the storm.

3. Thy bountiful care, what tongue can recite?
   It breathes in the air, it shines in the light.
   It streams from the hills, it descends to the plain,
   And sweetly distills in the dew and the rain.

4. Frail children of dust, and feeble as frail,
   In Thee do we trust, nor find Thee to fail.
   Thy mercies, how tender, how firm to the end,
   Our Maker, Defender, Redeemer and Friend.

The Old Rugged Cross

Words and Music by Rev. George Bennard

Additional Lyrics

2. Oh, that old rugged cross, so despised by the world,
   Has a wondrous attraction for me;
   For the dear Lamb of God left His glory above
   To bear it to dark Calvary.

3. In the old rugged cross, stained with blood so divine,
   Such a wonderful beauty I see;
   For 'twas on that old cross Jesus suffered and died
   To pardon and sanctify me.

4. To the old rugged cross I will ever be true,
   Its shame and reproach gladly bear;
   Then He'll call me someday to my home far away,
   Where His glory forever I'll share.

Praise to the Lord, the Almighty

Words by Joachim Neander
Translated by Catherine Winkworth
Music from *Erneuerten Gesangbuch*

Additional Lyrics

2. Praise to the Lord, who o'er all things so wondrously reigneth,
   Shelters thee under His wings, yea, so gently sustaineth.
   Hast thou not seen how all thy longings have been
   Granted in what He ordaineth?

3. Praise to the Lord, who doth prosper thy work and defend thee;
   Surely His goodness and mercy here daily attend thee.
   Ponder anew what the Almighty can do,
   If with His love He befriend thee.

4. Praise to the Lord! Oh, let all that is in me adore Him.
   All that hath life and breath, come now with praises before Him.
   Let the Amen sound from His people again;
   Gladly, for aye, we adore Him.

Rock of Ages

Words by August M. Toplady
v. 1, 2, 4 altered by Thomas Cotterill
Music by Thomas Hastings

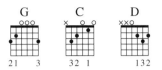

Additional Lyrics

2. Could my tears forever flow,
   Could my zeal no languor know,
   These for sin could not atone;
   Thou must save, and Thou alone.
   In my hand no price I bring;
   Simply to Thy cross I cling.

3. Nothing in my hand I bring;
   Simply to Thy cross I cling.
   Naked, come to Thee for dress;
   Helpless, look to Thee for grace.
   Foul, I to the fountain fly;
   Wash me, Savior, or I die.

4. While I draw this fleeting breath,
   When my eyes shall close in death,
   When I rise to worlds unknown
   And behold Thee on Thy throne,
   Rock of Ages, cleft for me,
   Let me hide myself in Thee.

Savior, Like a Shepherd Lead Us

Words from *Hymn for the Young*
Attributed to Dorothy A. Thrupp
Music by William B. Bradbury

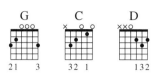

1. Sav - ior, like a shep-herd lead _____ us; _____ much we need Thy ten - der care.
2.–4. *See additional lyrics*

In Thy pleas-ant pas-tures feed _____ us, _____ for our use Thy folds pre - pare. Bless-ed

Je - sus, bless-ed Je - sus, Thou hast bought us, Thine we are. Bless-ed

Je - sus, bless-ed Je - sus, Thou hast bought us, Thine we are. still.

Additional Lyrics

2. We are Thine; do Thou befriend us,
   Be the guardian of our way.
   Keep Thy flock, from sin defend us,
   Seek us when we go astray.
   Blessed Jesus, blessed Jesus,
   Hear, O hear us when we pray.
   Blessed Jesus, blessed Jesus,
   Hear, O hear us when we pray.

3. Thou hast promised to receive us,
   Poor and sinful though we be.
   Thou hast mercy to relieve us,
   Grace to cleanse and pow'r to free.
   Blessed Jesus, blessed Jesus,
   Early let us turn to Thee.
   Blessed Jesus, blessed Jesus,
   Early let us turn to Thee.

4. Early let us seek Thy favor,
   Early let us do Thy will.
   Blessed Lord and only Savior,
   With Thy love our bosoms fill.
   Blessed Jesus, blessed Jesus,
   Thou hast loved us; love us still.
   Blessed Jesus, blessed Jesus,
   Thou hast loved us; love us still.

Stand Up, Stand Up for Jesus

Words by George Duffield, Jr.
Music by George J. Webb

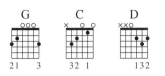

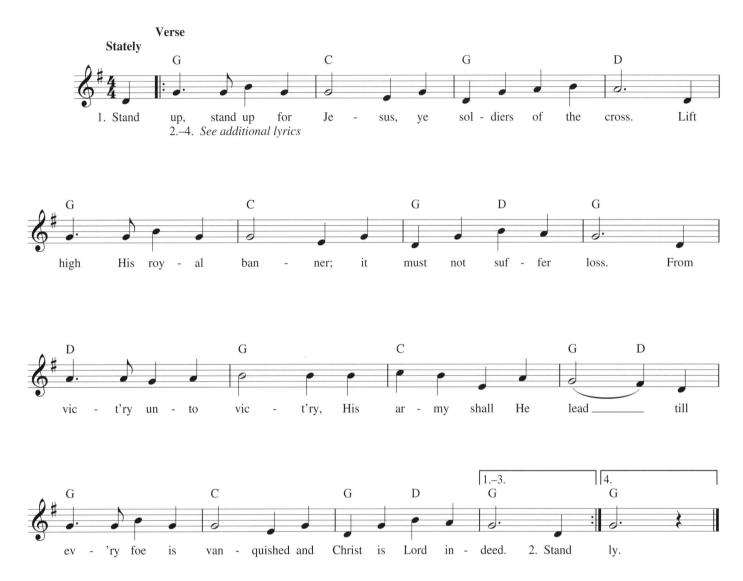

Additional Lyrics

2. Stand up, stand up for Jesus, the trumpet call obey;
   Forth to the mighty conflict in this His glorious day.
   Ye who are men, now serve Him against unnumbered foes.
   Let courage rise with danger, and strength to strength oppose.

3. Stand up, stand up for Jesus, stand in His strength alone.
   The arm of flesh will fail you; ye dare not trust your own.
   Put on the gospel armor, each piece put on with prayer.
   Where duty calls, or danger, be never wanting there.

4. Stand up, stand up for Jesus; the strife will not be long.
   This day, the noise of battle; the next, the victor's song.
   To him who overcometh, a crown of life shall be;
   He, with the King of glory, shall reign eternally.

Standing on the Promises

Words and Music by R. Kelso Carter

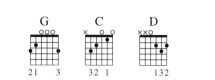

Verse

Bright Swing feel

1. Stand-ing on the prom-is-es of Christ my King. Through e - ter - nal a - ges let His
2.–4. *See additional lyrics*

prais - es ring. Glo - ry in the high - est, I will shout and sing,

Chorus

stand - ing on the prom - is - es of God. Stand - ing, stand - ing,

stand - ing on the prom - is - es of God my Sav - ior. Stand - ing,

stand - ing, I'm stand - ing on the prom - is - es of God. God.

Additional Lyrics

2. Standing on the promises that cannot fail,
When the howling storms of doubt and fear assail.
By the living word of God I shall prevail,
Standing on the promises of God.

3. Standing on the promises of Christ the Lord,
Bound to Him eternally by love's strong cord.
Overcoming daily with the Spirit's sword,
Standing on the promises of God.

4. Standing on the promises I cannot fall,
Listening ev'ry moment to the Spirit's call.
Resting in my Savior as my all in all,
Standing on the promises of God.

Take My Life and Let It Be

Words by Frances R. Havergal
Music by Henry A. César Malan

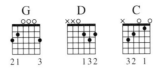

Additional Lyrics

2. Take my hands and let them move
   At the impulse of Thy love.
   Take my feet and let them be
   Swift and beautiful for Thee,
   Swift and beautiful for Thee.

3. Take my voice and let me sing
   Always, only for my King.
   Take my lips and let them be
   Filled with messages from Thee,
   Filled with messages from Thee.

4. Take my silver and my gold;
   Not a mite would I withhold.
   Take my intellect and use
   Ev'ry pow'r as Thou shalt choose,
   Ev'ry pow'r as Thou shalt choose.

5. Take my will and make it Thine;
   It shall be no longer mine.
   Take my heart; it is Thine own.
   It shall be Thy royal throne,
   It shall be Thy royal throne.

6. Take my love; my Lord, I pour
   At Thy feet its treasure store.
   Take myself, and I will be
   Ever, only, all for Thee.
   Ever, only, all for Thee.

This Is My Father's World

Words by Maltbie D. Babcock
Music by Franklin L. Sheppard

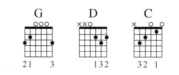

Additional Lyrics

2. This is my Father's world, the birds their carols raise.
   The morning light, the lily white declare their Maker's praise.
   This is my Father's world, He shines in all that's fair.
   In the rustling grass I hear Him pass, He speaks to me everywhere.

3. This is my Father's world, O let me ne'er forget
   That though the wrong seems oft so strong, God is the Ruler yet.
   This is my Father's world, the battle is not done.
   Jesus who died shall be satisfied, and earth and heav'n be one.

'Tis So Sweet to Trust in Jesus

Words by Louisa M.R. Stead
Music by William J. Kirkpatrick

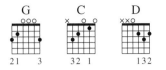

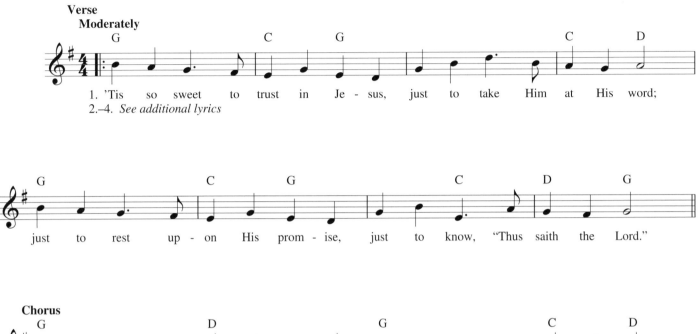

Additional Lyrics

2. O how sweet to trust in Jesus,
   Just to trust His cleansing blood,
   Just in simple faith to plunge me
   'Neath the healing, cleansing flood.

3. Yes, 'tis sweet to trust in Jesus,
   Just from sin and self to cease,
   Just from Jesus simply taking
   Life and rest and joy and peace.

4. I'm so glad I learned to trust Him,
   Precious Jesus, Savior, Friend;
   And I know that He is with me,
   Will be with me to the end.

What a Friend We Have in Jesus

Words by Joseph M. Scriven
Music by Charles C. Converse

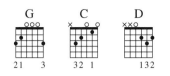

Additional Lyrics

2. Have we trials and temptations?
   Is there trouble anywhere?
   We should never be discouraged;
   Take it to the Lord in prayer.
   Can we find a friend so faithful,
   Who will all our sorrows share?
   Jesus knows our ev'ry weakness;
   Take it to the Lord in prayer.

3. Are we weak and heavy-laden,
   Cumbered with a load of care?
   Precious Savior, still our refuge;
   Take it to the Lord in prayer.
   Do thy friends despise, forsake thee?
   Take it to the Lord in prayer.
   In His arms He'll take and shield thee;
   Thou wilt find a solace there.

When I Survey the Wondrous Cross

Words by Isaac Watts
Music arranged by Lowell Mason
Based on Plainsong

Additional Lyrics

2. Forbid it, Lord, that I should boast,
   Save in the death of Christ, my God.
   All the vain things that charm me most,
   I sacrifice them to His blood.

3. See, from His head, His hands, His feet,
   Sorrow and love flow mingled down.
   Did e'er such love and sorrow meet,
   Or thorns compose so rich a crown?

4. Were the whole realm of nature mine,
   That were a present far too small.
   Love so amazing, so divine,
   Demands my soul, my life, my all.

christian guitar songbooks

ACOUSTIC GUITAR WORSHIP

30 praise song favorites arranged for guitar, including: Awesome God • Forever • I Could Sing of Your Love Forever • Lord, Reign in Me • Open the Eyes of My Heart • and more.
00699672 Solo Guitar...$14.99

FAVORITE HYMNS FOR SOLO GUITAR

Amazing Grace • Christ the Lord Is Risen Today • For the Beauty of the Earth • Holy, Holy, Holy • In the Garden • Let Us Break Bread Together • O for a Thousand Tongues to Sing • Were You There? • What a Friend We Have in Jesus • When I Survey the Wondrous Cross • more.
00699275 Fingerstyle Guitar $12.99

FINGERPICKING HYMNS

Abide with Me • Amazing Grace • Beneath the Cross of Jesus • Come, Thou Fount of Every Blessing • For the Beauty of the Earth • A Mighty Fortress Is Our God • Rock of Ages • and more.
00699688 Solo Guitar..$9.99

FINGERPICKING WORSHIP

Agnus Dei • Amazing Grace (My Chains Are Gone) • How Deep the Father's Love for Us • How Great Is Our God • I Worship You, Almighty God • More Precious Than Silver • There Is a Redeemer • We Fall Down • and more, plus an easy introduction to basic fingerstyle guitar.
00700554 Solo Guitar...$10.99

GOSPEL GUITAR SONGBOOK

Includes notes & tab for fingerpicking and Travis picking arrangements of 15 favorites: Amazing Grace • Blessed Assurance • Do Lord • I've Got Peace Like a River • Just a Closer Walk with Thee • O Happy Day • Precious Memories • Rock of Ages • Swing Low, Sweet Chariot • There Is Power in the Blood • When the Saints Go Marching In • and more!
00695372 Guitar with Notes & Tab $9.95

GOSPEL HYMNS

Amazing Grace • At the Cross • Blessed Assurance • Higher Ground • I've Got Peace like a River • In the Garden • Love Lifted Me • The Old Rugged Cross • Rock of Ages • What a Friend We Have in Jesus • When the Saints Go Marching In • Wondrous Love • and more.
00700463
Lyrics/Chord Symbols/Guitar Chord Diagrams........$14.99

HYMNS FOR CLASSICAL GUITAR

Amazing Grace • Be Thou My Vision • Come, Thou Fount of Every Blessing • For the Beauty of the Earth • Joyful, Joyful, We Adore Thee • My Faith Looks up to Thee • Rock of Ages • What a Friend We Have in Jesus • and more.
00701898 Solo Guitar...$14.99

HYMNS FOR SOLO JAZZ GUITAR

Book/Online Video

Abide with Me • Amazing Grace • Blessed Assurance • God Is So Good • Just a Closer Walk with Thee • Londonderry Air • Oh How I Love Jesus • Softly and Tenderly • Sweet Hour of Prayer • What a Friend We Have in Jesus.
00153842 Solo Guitar...$19.99

MODERN WORSHIP – GUITAR CHORD SONGBOOK

Amazed • Amazing Grace (My Chains Are Gone) • At the Cross • Beautiful One • Everlasting God • How Can I Keep from Singing • I Am Free • Let God Arise • Let My Words Be Few (I'll Stand in Awe of You) • Made to Worship • Mighty to Save • Nothing but the Blood • Offering • Sing to the King • Today Is the Day • Your Name • and more.
00701801
Lyrics/Chord Symbols/Guitar Chord Diagrams........$16.99

PRAISE & WORSHIP – STRUM & SING

This inspirational collection features 25 favorites for guitarists to strum and sing. Includes chords and lyrics for: Amazing Grace (My Chains Are Gone) • Cornerstone • Everlasting God • Forever • The Heart of Worship • How Great Is Our God • In Christ Alone • Mighty to Save • 10,000 Reasons (Bless the Lord) • This I Believe • We Fall Down • and more.
00152381 Guitar/Vocal..$12.99

SACRED SONGS FOR CLASSICAL GUITAR

Bind Us Together • El Shaddai • Here I Am, Lord • His Name Is Wonderful • How Great Thou Art • I Walked Today Where Jesus Walked • On Eagle's Wings • Thou Art Worthy • and more.
00702426 Guitar..$14.99

SUNDAY SOLOS FOR GUITAR

Great Is Thy Faithfulness • Here I Am to Worship • How Great Is Our God • Joyful, Joyful, We Adore Thee • There Is a Redeemer • We Fall Down • What a Friend We Have in Jesus • and more!
00703083 Guitar..$14.99

TOP CHRISTIAN HITS – STRUM & SING GUITAR

Good Good Father (Chris Tomlin) • Greater (MercyMe) • Holy Spirit (Francesca Battistelli) • I Am (Crowder) • Same Power (Jeremy Camp) • This Is Amazing Grace (Phil Wickham) • and more.
00156331 Guitar/Vocal..$12.99

THE WORSHIP GUITAR ANTHOLOGY – VOLUME 1

This collection contains melody, lyrics & chords for 100 contemporary favorites, such as: Beautiful One • Forever • Here I Am to Worship • Hosanna (Praise Is Rising) • How He Loves • In Christ Alone • Mighty to Save • Our God • Revelation Song • Your Grace Is Enough • and dozens more.
00101864 Melody/Lyrics/Chords...........................$16.99

WORSHIP SOLOS FOR FINGERSTYLE GUITAR

Ancient Words • Before the Throne of God Above • Broken Vessels (Amazing Grace) • Cornerstone • Good Good Father • Great Are You Lord • Holy Spirit • I Will Rise • King of My Heart • Lord, I Need You • O Come to the Altar • O Praise the Name (Anastasis) • Oceans (Where Feet May Fail) • 10,000 Reasons (Bless the Lord) • Your Name.
00276831 Guitar..$14.99

TOP WORSHIP SONGS FOR GUITAR

Amazing Grace (My Chains Are Gone) • Because He Lives, Amen • Cornerstone • Forever (We Sing Hallelujah) • Good Good Father • Holy Spirit • Jesus Messiah • Lead Me to the Cross • Our God • Revelation Song • This Is Amazing Grace • We Believe • Your Grace Is Enough • and more.
00160854 Melody/Lyrics/Chords...........................$12.99

Prices, contents and availability subject to change without notice.